PUDDINGS
& DESSERTS

PUDDINGS & DESSERTS

Traditional recipes for tempting puddings and desserts

CONTENTS

TECHNIQUES 6

Guide to symbols

The recipes in this book are accompanied by symbols that alert you to important information.

 Tells you how many people the recipe serves, or how much is produced.

 Indicates how much time you will need to prepare and cook a dish. Next to this symbol you will also find out if additional time is required for such things as marinating, standing, proving, or cooling. You need to read the recipe to find out exactly how much extra time is needed.

 Alerts you to what has to be done before you can begin to cook the recipe, or to parts of the recipe that take a long time to complete.

 Denotes that special equipment is required. Where possible, alternatives are given.

 Accompanies freezing information.

Techniques

Make ice cream

Ice cream can be easily made by hand, or with a machine for a finer texture.

By hand

1 Split 2 vanilla pods, and scrape out and reserve the seeds. Add the pods to a pan with 500ml (16fl oz) double cream, and bring to boil. Add 75g (2½oz) golden caster sugar, and stir until dissolved.

2 In a bowl, whisk 4 egg yolks until well combined, then strain the warm cream mixture into the eggs, stirring all the time. Add the reserved vanilla seeds, and stir.

3 Pour the ice cream mixture into a metal loaf tin or plastic tub. Leave to cool completely.

4 Once cool, put into the freezer. When frozen, double-wrap with cling film and freeze for up to 3 months.

With an ice cream machine

1 Prepare a custard (see steps 1 and 2, opposite) and cool in a bowl set over a separate bowl of ice. Stir the mixture continuously to prevent a skin forming on the surface.

2 Pour the custard mixture into an ice cream machine. Continue churning or processing until thick and smooth, then place in a container and freeze until firm.

Make granita
Combine sugar, fruit juice, and water (or red or white wine) to make a syrup that can be frozen to create a light and refreshing dessert.

1 Slowly bring the ingredients to boil, reduce heat, and simmer for 2–3 minutes, stirring. Cool, pour into a shallow baking tray, and freeze. When half-frozen, use a fork to break up the chunks.

2 Break up the crystals once or twice more until evenly frozen. Remove from the freezer 5–10 minutes before serving, to thaw slightly. Scrape up the frozen granita and serve in pre-chilled glasses.

Make fruit sorbet

Lighter than ice cream and a perfect palate cleanser.
You can use any berries.

1 Combine 75g (2½ oz) of sugar in a pan with 60ml (2fl oz) water. Simmer gently for 5–10 minutes, until the sugar has dissolved, and the mixture has thickened.

2 Put 1kg (2¼lb) of strawberries in a food processor, and whiz until puréed. (Alternatively, pass them through a sieve to remove the seeds.) Pour the syrup mixture into the puréed strawberries and stir.

3 Pour the mixture into a freezerproof container – the shallower the better (it will freeze quicker). Leave to cool completely, then put into the freezer.

4 When frozen, remove and stir well to break up any ice crystals, then put back into the freezer. Sorbet is best eaten within a few days, as the fresh fruit taste starts to fade after a while.

Make lacy crêpes
Making these crêpes involves two essentials – the right temperature and the perfect batter. See p14 for ingredient quantities.

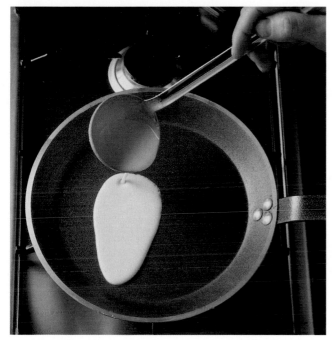

1 Heat a little clarified butter in a crêpe pan and pour off any excess. Holding the pan at an angle, pour in a little of the batter.

2 Tilt and swirl the pan as you pour in more batter to thinly and evenly coat the base of the pan.

3 When the crêpe has cooked to a pale gold colour underneath, use a long spatula to loosen and flip the crêpe back into the pan.

4 Cook until the second side is golden. Place on baking parchment with a layer between each finished crêpe. Continue cooking the rest of the batter.

Make French meringue

This meringue will be caramelized and crunchy on the outside and soft and yielding inside. For ingredient quantities, see p44.

1 In a large mixing bowl, whisk together the egg whites, half of the sugar, and the vanilla seeds at a moderate speed.

2 Continue whisking until the mixture becomes smooth, shiny, and firm.

3 Using a rubber spatula, gradually fold the rest of the sugar into the egg mixture, taking care not to lose any of the volume.

4 Shape the meringue (see opposite), then bake it so that the centre is just golden. Turn off the oven. Prop the oven door open and leave to dry for at least 8 hours, or overnight.

Shape meringue

A pastry bag can be used to shape meringue or to apply it as a topping to a tart. Prepare a baking tray with parchment before shaping.

For discs or layers, using a pastry bag with a star tip, pipe the meringue in a spiral beginning in the centre and moving outward. Bake for 1 hour 20 minutes, then let dry.

For shells, using a pastry bag with a round tip, pipe the meringue into equal-sized globes and bake for 1 hour 10 minutes, then let dry.

For fingers, using a pastry bag with a round tip, pipe the meringue into thin, even sticks, and dust them with icing sugar. Bake for 30–35 minutes, then let dry.

To cover a tart, using a pastry bag with a star tip, pipe the meringue over top of the tart in attractive peaks. Dust with icing sugar and place under a hot grill for a few minutes, or until golden brown.

Make caramel

The trick to making good caramel is to prevent the sugar from crystallizing; add some liquid glucose to help achieve this. This recipe makes 500ml (16fl oz).

Make syrup

1 Combine 150ml (5fl oz) of water, 350g (12 oz) caster sugar, and 115g (4 oz) liquid glucose in a heavy saucepan over a low heat, stirring often with a wooden spoon. Wipe the side of the pan with a wet pastry brush to stop the sugar crystallizing.

2 Once the sugar has dissolved, bring the liquid to the boil. When the caramel becomes golden brown in colour and is just thick enough to coat the back of a teaspoon, stop the cooking at once by plunging the entire pan into a large bowl of iced water.

Make sauce

Remove the pan from the iced water after a minute, but while the syrup is still warm. Whisk in a knob of softened butter and softly whipped cream or crème fraîche to your taste. Whisk until the sauce is thick, slightly sticky, and smooth. Return the pan to a low heat, and bring to a gentle boil, or until the sauce temperature reaches 103°C (217°F). You can measure the temperature of the caramel accurately by using a sugar thermometer.

Prepare chocolate

Chill the chocolate before cutting and grating, as the warmth of your hands will quickly melt it.

For chopping, break the chocolate into small pieces, then chill the pieces in the freezer for a few minutes. Place on a cutting board and use a sharp knife to chop using a rocking motion.

For grating, rub chilled chocolate against the face of the grater, using the widest holes. If the chocolate begins to melt, chill it again in the freezer and continue grating once it has hardened.

To melt chocolate, gently simmer some water in a pan. Place chopped chocolate in a heatproof bowl and set it over the water. Let the chocolate melt, then it stir with a wooden spoon until smooth.

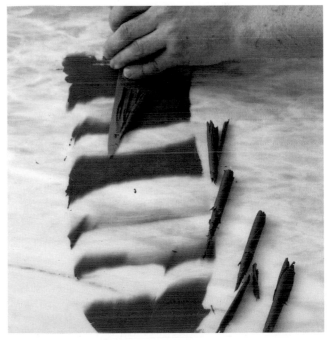

For curls, spread soft or melted chocolate on to a cool marble surface. Use the blade of a chef's knife to scrape the chocolate into curls.

Crêpes flambées

This twist on a classic French dessert makes a spectacular end to any dinner.

INGREDIENTS

100g (3½ oz) plain flour
2 eggs, beaten
sunflower oil or groundnut oil
pinch of salt
250ml (9fl oz) milk
butter, for frying

For the flambé sauce

60g (2 oz) unsalted butter
100g (3½ oz) maple syrup
juice and grated zest of 2 oranges
4 tbsp brandy or orange liqueur

METHOD

1 To make the crêpe batter, put the flour into a large bowl and make a well in the centre. Add the eggs, with oil and salt to taste, and gradually whisk in the milk to make a smooth, thin batter.

2 Heat a 23cm (9in) crêpe pan over a medium heat until hot. Add a knob of butter to coat the base evenly. Ladle in the crêpe batter to cover the base thinly, tilting the pan to spread the batter. Cook for 1–2 minutes, or until the base is golden. Flip the crêpe over and cook for a further minute, or until golden (see p9). Fold the crêpe into quarters in the pan, then remove it, set aside, and repeat to make the rest of the crêpes.

3 To prepare the flambé sauce, melt the butter in a separate pan over a medium heat. Add the maple syrup, orange juice, and zest and leave to bubble for 5 minutes, stirring, until the syrup dissolves and the sauce thickens slightly.

4 Add the crêpes one by one into the sauce. Pour the brandy into a clean ladle and tip it into a flame to ignite. Immediately pour the flaming sauce over the crêpes and serve hot.

serves 4

prep 25–35 mins,
• cook 15–20 mins

23cm (9in)
crêpe pan

freeze, interleaved
with greaseproof paper,
for up to 3 months

Lemon and sugar crêpes

A favourite treat for breakfast, lunch, or tea, these simple pancakes are a family favourite.

INGREDIENTS

115g (4 oz) plain flour
¼ tsp salt
1 egg
300ml (10fl oz) milk
about 3 tbsp vegetable oil, for frying
lemon wedges and caster sugar, to serve

METHOD

1 Sift the flour and salt into a large bowl and make a well in the centre. Add the egg and milk and whisk together, gradually drawing in flour from the sides, to make a smooth, thin batter. Slowly add the remaining milk, beating until smooth. Leave to stand for 10 minutes.
2 Preheat the oven to its lowest setting. Heat the crêpe pan over a high heat until hot. Pour in enough vegetable oil to coat the bottom of the pan, swirl around, then pour off the excess.
3 Ladle 3 tbsp of the batter into the centre of the pan and tilt so that it covers the base thinly. Cook the crêpe for 1–2 minutes, or until small bubbles appear. Slide a palette knife underneath and flip over, then continue cooking for 30 seconds, or until golden. (See p9 for step-by-step technique.)
4 Remove and keep warm in the oven. Repeat until all the batter has been used.
5 Serve hot, sprinkled with sugar and lemon juice.

serves 4

prep 5 mins, plus standing
• cook 10 mins

18cm (7in) crêpe pan

freeze, interleaved with greaseproof paper, for up to 3 months

Cherry clafoutis

This French favourite can be enjoyed warm or at room temperature.

INGREDIENTS

750g (1lb 10 oz) cherries
3 tbsp kirsch
75g (2½ oz) caster sugar
butter, for greasing
4 large eggs
1 vanilla pod, split in half lengthways
100g (3½ oz) plain flour, sifted
300ml (10fl oz) milk
pinch of salt

METHOD

1 Toss the cherries with the kirsch and 2 tablespoons of the sugar in a medium-sized bowl, and leave to stand for 30 minutes.

2 Meanwhile, preheat the oven to 200°C (400°F/Gas 6). Butter the flan tin, and set aside.

3 Strain the liquid from the cherries and beat it with the eggs, the seeds from the vanilla pod, and the remaining sugar. Slowly beat in the flour, then add the milk and salt, and mix to make a smooth batter.

4 Arrange the cherries in the flan tin, then pour the batter over. Place in the oven and bake for 35–45 minutes, or until the top is browned and the centre is firm to the touch.

5 Dust with sifted icing sugar and allow to cool on a wire rack. Serve warm or at room temperature. This is delicious served with thick cream, crème fraîche, or vanilla ice cream.

 serves 6

 prep 12 mins, plus standing • cook 35–45 mins

 25cm (10in) flan tin

Pineapple and syrup upside-down pudding

This sunshine-coloured pudding is baked 'upside-down' so the pineapples are on top when it is turned out.

INGREDIENTS

2–3 tbsp golden syrup
400ml can pineapple rings, drained
150g (5½ oz) butter
125g (4½ oz) golden caster sugar
2 eggs
175g (6 oz) self-raising flour, sifted
1–2 tbsp milk

METHOD

1 Preheat the oven to 180°C (350°F/Gas 4). Grease the ovenproof dish. Drizzle in the golden syrup to cover the base, then top with the pineapple rings, and put to one side.

2 Place the butter and sugar in a bowl, then whisk with an electric hand whisk until pale and creamy. Mix in the eggs, one at a time, adding a little of the flour after each one. Fold in the remaining flour, then add the milk a little at a time until the mixture drops easily off the beaters. Pour the mixture over the pineapples and bake in the oven for 40–50 minutes, or until golden brown and springy to the touch. Serve hot from the oven.

serves 4–6

prep 10 mins,
• cook 50 mins

1.2-litre (2-pint) ovenproof dish • electric hand whisk or mixer

freeze the pudding in its dish, wrapped in cling film, for up to 3 months

Banoffee pie

Always a hit, this dessert's name derives from its delicious filling of fresh bananas and toffee sauce.

INGREDIENTS

20cm ready-made tart case

200g (7 oz) ready-made thick caramel
 sauce (such as Dulce de leche)

2–3 ripe bananas

300ml (10fl oz) double cream
 or whipping cream

25g (scant 1 oz) dark chocolate

METHOD

1 Place the tart case on a serving plate. Spoon in the caramel sauce and spread evenly. Slice the bananas and scatter over the top.

2 Put the cream in a bowl and whisk with an electric hand whisk until soft peaks form, then spoon over the bananas. Grate the chocolate over the top (see p13) and serve.

serves 8

prep 15 mins

electric
hand whisk

Pineapple with mint

This fruit platter makes a refreshing end to any meal.

INGREDIENTS

1 large ripe pineapple
1 pomegranate
finely grated zest and juice of 1 lime
25g (scant 1 oz) mint leaves, chopped
2 tbsp light soft brown sugar

METHOD

1 Using a sharp knife, cut away the skin from the pineapple. Cut the flesh into quarters, remove and discard the woody core, and slice thinly. Arrange on a serving plate.
2 Cut the pomegranate in half and remove the seeds, discarding all the membranes. Scatter the seeds over the pineapple slices and pour the lime juice over the fruit.
3 Place the mint in a small bowl, add the lime zest and sugar, and mix well. Scatter evenly over the fruit, then chill in the refrigerator for at least 1 hour. Bring back to room temperature to serve.

serves 4

prep 20 mins,
plus chilling

Zabaglione

This Italian pudding was invented by mistake in the 17th century when wine was poured into egg custard.

INGREDIENTS

4 egg yolks
4 tbsp caster sugar
8 tbsp Marsala
finely grated zest of 1 orange
8 sponge fingers or biscotti, to serve

METHOD

1 Bring a large saucepan of water to the boil, then lower the heat to simmer.
2 Put the egg yolks, sugar, Marsala, and half the orange zest into a large glass or china bowl and place on top of the pan of simmering water. Start to whisk immediately, using a balloon whisk. Keep whisking for 5–10 minutes, or until the mixture is pale, thick, fluffy, and warmed through.
3 Pour into 4 cocktail glasses and decorate with the remaining orange zest; serve immediately with sponge fingers or biscotti.

serves 4

prep 5 mins,
• cook 10 mins

Classic pavlova

This classic meringue dessert is named after Russian ballerina Anna Pavlova but credit for inventing it is claimed by both Australia and New Zealand.

INGREDIENTS

6 egg whites, at room temperature
pinch of salt
350g (12 oz) caster sugar
2 tsp cornflour
1 tsp vinegar
300ml (10fl oz) double cream
strawberries, kiwi fruit, and passion
  fruit, to decorate

METHOD

1 Preheat the oven to 180°C (350°F/Gas 4). Line a baking tray with greaseproof paper. Put the egg whites in a large, clean, grease-free bowl with a pinch of salt. Whisk until stiff, then start whisking in the sugar 1 tablespoon at a time, whisking well after each addition. Continue whisking until the egg whites are stiff and glossy, then whisk in the cornflour and vinegar.

2 Spoon the meringue on to the baking tray and spread to form a 20cm (8in) circle. Bake for 5 minutes, then reduce the oven to 140°C (275°F/Gas 1) and cook for a further 1 hour and 15 minutes, or until the outside is crisp. Allow it to cool completely before transferring to a serving plate.

3 Whip the cream until it holds its shape, then spoon it on to the meringue base. Decorate with the fruit and serve.

serves 6

prep 15 mins,
plus cooling
• cook 1 hr 20 mins

Raspberry crème brûlée

Fresh raspberries make this classic French dessert extra special.

INGREDIENTS

200g (7 oz) fresh raspberries
4 large egg yolks
8 tbsp golden caster sugar
560ml (18fl oz) double cream
1 tsp pure vanilla extract

METHOD

1 Divide the raspberries among the ramekins. Put the egg yolks and 2 tablespoons of the sugar in a large bowl and whisk with an electric hand whisk until the mixture begins to thicken and becomes pale and creamy.

2 Heat the cream gently in a pan for 5 minutes. Do not let it boil. Remove from the heat, stir in the pure vanilla extract, and allow to cool for 5 minutes.

3 Slowly add the warm cream to the egg mixture a little at a time, whisking constantly. When it's all in, pour the mixture back into the pan, and cook over a low heat for a couple of minutes, stirring all the time with a wooden spoon until thick. Do not allow to boil. Pour the custard into the ramekins and allow to cool completely. Transfer to the refrigerator to set for a couple of hours or overnight.

4 When ready to serve, sprinkle the tops of the custards evenly with the remaining sugar and place under a hot grill until the sugar bubbles and turns golden brown. Alternatively, use a cook's blowtorch, making sweeping movements with the flame until the sugar starts to caramelize. Allow the topping to harden for 20 minutes before serving.

serves 6

prep 10 mins, plus chilling • cook 45 mins

chill for at least 2 hrs, or overnight if possible

6 ramekins • electric hand whisk

Mini summer puddings

Summer pudding is usually one big dessert, but this recipe gives guests an individual pudding all to themselves.

INGREDIENTS

about 9 slices white bread, crusts removed

700g (1lb 9oz) mixed summer berries and currants

75g (2½ oz) caster sugar, or to taste

icing sugar, to dust (optional)

METHOD

1 Line the pudding basins with the bread, tearing the slices into pieces to fit. Remember to reserve some bread to fit the tops after the fruit has been added. Make sure the basins are well lined – any gaps will cause the puddings to collapse when turned out.

2 Put the fruit in a pan with caster sugar and 250ml (9fl oz) water. Bring to the boil, stirring until the sugar dissolves. Simmer gently for 5 minutes, or until the berries start to soften and release their juices. Test for sweetness and add a little more sugar if needed. Spoon some of the juice into the basins so the bread starts to soak it up. Divide the berries among the basins, pushing them down to pack in as many as possible and letting the bread absorb the juice – no white bread should show when the puddings are turned out. Packing in as many fruits as possible will prevent the puddings collapsing. Cover the berry filling with the remaining bread, and then spoon over the last of the juice until no white bread is visible.

3 Cover each basin tightly with cling film and leave to chill in the refrigerator for at least 2 hours. To serve, turn out onto individual serving plates. Dust with icing sugar before serving, if you like.

serves 6 | prep 30 mins, plus chilling | chill for at least 2 hrs, or overnight if possible | 6 x 200ml (7fl oz) pudding basins | freeze the puddings in their basins, covered with cling film, for up to 2 months

Hot orange sweet soufflés

Hot soufflés are quite easy to make, but they need a little care. This is a basic soufflé, flavoured with orange zest.

INGREDIENTS

50g (1¾ oz) butter, melted
60g (2 oz) caster sugar, plus extra for
   dusting
45g (1½ oz) plain flour
300ml (10fl oz) milk
finely grated zest of 2 oranges
2 tbsp orange juice
3 eggs, separated
1 egg white

METHOD

1 Preheat the oven to 200°C (400°F/Gas 6). Put a baking tray in the oven.
2 Brush the ramekins with melted butter, then dust their insides with sugar, making sure there are no gaps.
3 Add the flour to the remaining melted butter and cook over a low heat for 1 minute. Remove from the heat and gradually add the milk. Return to the heat and bring slowly to the boil, stirring all the time. Simmer for 1–2 minutes, then remove from the heat again and add the orange zest and juice, and all but 1 teaspoon of the sugar.
4 Add the egg yolks to the sauce, beating in well. Whisk the whites to medium peaks and beat in the remaining 1 teaspoon of sugar. Mix 1 tablespoon of egg whites into the egg yolk mixture to loosen it, then fold in the rest of the egg whites.
5 Pour the mixture into the ramekins, scraping it away from the top of each dish with a small knife. Place on the hot baking tray and bake for 12–15 minutes, or until the puddings are golden and risen, but still a little runny in the centre.

 serves 4

 prep 20 mins,
• cook 12–15 mins

 4 small ramekins

 freeze, uncooked,
in the ramekins
for up to 1 month

Sticky toffee and banana pudding

A lovely winter pudding that is as fast to prepare as it is sure to be consumed.

INGREDIENTS

115g (4 oz) butter
115g (4 oz) light muscovado sugar
200ml (7fl oz) double cream
6 tbsp maple syrup
225g (8 oz) ginger cake, sliced
2 large bananas
60g (2 oz) pecan nuts, chopped

METHOD

1 Preheat the oven to 190°C (375°F/Gas 5). Place the butter, sugar, cream, and maple syrup in a small pan and heat gently, stirring constantly, until smooth.
2 Lightly grease a 20 x 30cm (8 x 12in) ovenproof dish. Arrange the cake and bananas in the dish, pour the sauce over, and scatter the pecans over the top. Bake for 10 minutes, or until the toffee sauce is bubbling.

serves 6

prep 5 mins,
• cook 10 mins

20 x 30cm (8 x 12in)
ovenproof dish

Chocolate mousse

For the ultimate chocolate sensation, this is best made with dark chocolate containing at least 70 per cent cocoa solids.

INGREDIENTS

100g (3½ oz) 70 per cent dark chocolate,
   broken up
1 tbsp milk
2 eggs, separated
35g (1¼ oz) caster sugar
150ml (5fl oz) double cream
dark chocolate, grated or curled to serve
   (optional)

METHOD

1 Place the chocolate and milk in a heatproof bowl over a pan of simmering water. When the chocolate has melted, stir until combined, remove from the heat, and allow to cool slightly.
2 Place the egg yolks and sugar in a large bowl and whisk until thick and creamy. Then whisk in the chocolate mixture.
3 Whip the cream in a bowl until stiff. Gently fold in the chocolate mixture until combined, taking care not to overmix. Whisk the egg whites until stiff, and gently fold into the chocolate mixture.
4 Spoon into individual dishes and refrigerate for at least 2 hours. If you like the mousse soft, take it out of the refrigerator and let it warm to room temperature before serving. Decorate with grated chocolate or chocolate curls, if you like (see p13).

serves 6

prep 20 mins,
plus chilling
• cook 20 mins

Coeur à la crème

These delicious little puddings are traditionally made in heart-shaped china moulds.

INGREDIENTS

225g (8 oz) cottage cheese, drained and
  sieved
300ml (10fl oz) double cream
60g (2 oz) icing sugar
1 tsp pure vanilla extract
2 egg whites
single cream, to serve
fresh berries, to serve

METHOD

1 Mix the sieved cottage cheese, cream, sugar, and vanilla extract together. Whisk the egg whites until they form peaks. Fold into the cheese mixture.
2 Fill the coeur à la crème moulds with the mixture and cover with cling film. Place in the refrigerator on a wire rack over a plate or tray to drain through the perforated holes, and leave for 2–3 days.
3 To serve, carefully invert the puddings on to plates. Serve with single cream and fresh berries.

serves 4

prep 20 mins,
plus draining

prepare 2–3 days in
advance to ensure
proper draining

4 coeur à la
crème moulds

Blackberry and apple sponge

Make this lovely, warming autumn dessert when the weather gets cooler.

INGREDIENTS

125g (4½ oz) butter, at room
   temperature
125g (4½ oz) caster sugar
2 large eggs
175g (6 oz) self-raising flour, sifted
2 Bramley apples, peeled, cored, and
   roughly chopped
250g (9 oz) blackberries
2 tbsp caster sugar
icing sugar, to dust (optional)

METHOD

1 Preheat the oven to 180°C (350°F/Gas 4). In a bowl, mix the butter and sugar together
   with an electric hand whisk or mixer until pale and creamy. Beat in the eggs one at a
   time, adding 1 tablespoon of the flour after each egg. Mix in the remaining flour and set
   aside. Put the apple and blackberries in the ovenproof dish, then stir in the caster sugar
   along with 2 tablespoons cold water. Spoon the sponge mixture over the top, and
   smooth the surface.
2 Bake for 50 minutes, or until golden brown and firm to the touch – a skewer inserted
   into the sponge should come out clean. Serve hot with a dusting of icing sugar, if using.

serves 6

prep 20 mins,
• cook 50 mins

electric hand
whisk or mixer •
1.2-litre (2-pint)
ovenproof dish

freeze in its dish,
wrapped in foil, for
up to 3 months

Floating islands

In this delicious French dessert, *Iles Flottantes*, meringues poached in milk float on top of vanilla-flavoured custard.

INGREDIENTS

450ml (15fl oz) milk
300ml (10fl oz) double cream
175g (6 oz) caster sugar, plus 2 tsp extra
1 vanilla pod (optional)
2 tsp cornflour

4 egg yolks
1 tsp pure vanilla extract
3 egg whites
2 tbsp grated chocolate, to serve

METHOD

1 Place half the milk in a saucepan with the cream, 2 teaspoons of sugar, and the vanilla pod, if using. Bring to a simmer, remove from the heat, and leave to stand for 30 minutes so the flavours infuse. Remove the vanilla pod.

2 Put the cornflour into a bowl and mix in a little cold milk. Pour the infused milk into the bowl, stirring all the time. Put the milk back in the pan and bring to the boil, stirring constantly. Simmer for 2 minutes to cook the cornflour.

3 Whisk the egg yolks in a bowl and pour the hot milk over them, whisking all the time. The custard should be thick enough to coat the back of a spoon. If not, place over a gentle heat and, stirring constantly, allow it to thicken. Do not boil or it will curdle. Add the pure vanilla extract at this stage. Pour into a bowl then cover with dampened greaseproof paper to prevent a skin forming, and leave to chill.

4 Put the remaining milk and 300ml (10fl oz) water in a deep frying pan, bring to the boil, then reduce the heat so it simmers.

5 Whisk the egg whites until they form stiff peaks. Gradually whisk in the rest of the sugar to make the meringue mixture. Carefully place 3 or 4 tablespoons of the meringue mixture into the simmering milk and water to cook. Do not put more than 4 at a time into the pan as they will almost double in size. Cook for 1 minute, turning once. Lift out with a slotted spoon and put on a tea towel to drain. Repeat with the remaining meringues, set aside, and let cool.

6 Divide the custard between serving dishes and top with 1 or 2 floating islands. Just before serving, sprinkle the islands with the grated chocolate.

serves 4

prep 15 mins,
plus standing
• cook 30 mins

Brown sugar meringues

These sweet treats will be loved by children and adults alike. Brown sugar adds a lovely caramel flavour to the meringues.

INGREDIENTS
4 egg whites
200g (7 oz) soft brown sugar

METHOD
1 Preheat the oven to 130°C (250°F/Gas ½). Whisk the egg whites until stiff in a clean bowl. Whisk in the sugar, 2 tablespoons at a time.
2 Line 2 baking trays with greaseproof paper. Using a dessert spoon, place spoonfuls of the meringue mixture on to the trays. Bake for 1 hour, or until crisp on the outside and slightly chewy inside (see step-by-step technique on p10). Delicious served with whipped double cream and drizzled with melted dark chocolate.

makes 36 small
meringues

prep 20 mins
• cook 1 hr

Quindim

This sweet, creamy, and very rich dessert is a popular party dish in Brazil.

INGREDIENTS

100g (3½ oz) caster sugar

4 egg yolks

2 tbsp grated fresh coconut

60ml (2fl oz) coconut milk

grated fresh coconut, toasted, to serve

METHOD

1 Preheat the oven to 180°C (350°F/Gas 4). Whisk the sugar and egg yolks in a bowl until light and creamy. Add the fresh coconut and coconut milk, and stir until evenly combined. Spoon into the ramekins.

2 Stand the ramekins in a roasting tin and pour in enough warm water to come halfway up the sides of the dishes.

3 Bake for 25–30 minutes, or until set. Lift the dishes out of the tin, leave to cool, and then chill for at least 3–4 hours before serving.

serves 4

prep 15 mins,
plus chilling
• cook 25–30 mins

chill for at
least 3–4 hrs

4 small ramekins

Lemon meringue roulade

The traditional roulade filling is given a new twist in this impressive dessert.

INGREDIENTS

5 egg whites
225g (8 oz) caster sugar
½ tsp white wine vinegar
1 tsp cornflour
½ tsp pure vanilla extract
250ml (9fl oz) double cream
4 tbsp ready-made lemon curd
icing sugar, for dusting

METHOD

1 Preheat the oven to 180°C (350°F/Gas 4) and line the baking tin with greaseproof paper.
2 Whisk the egg whites until stiff peaks form. Continue whisking at a slower speed and gradually add the caster sugar, a little at a time. Gently fold in the vinegar, cornflour, and vanilla extract.
3 Spread the mixture into the tin and bake in the centre of the oven for 15 minutes. Remove from the oven and allow to cool.
4 Meanwhile, whisk the cream until thick and fold in the lemon curd until blended.
5 Turn the cooled roulade out onto another piece of greaseproof paper and spread the lemon cream evenly over the roulade. Roll the meringue and keep covered and chilled. Slice the roulade when ready to serve.

serves 8

prep 30 mins
• cook 15 mins

25 × 35 cm
(10 × 14in) shallow
baking tin or
Swiss roll tin

freeze for up to
2 months

Berries with citrus syrup

Juicy seasonal berries are made even more luscious with a sweet lemon-orange syrup.

INGREDIENTS
500g (1lb 2oz) mixed red berries,
    such as raspberries, strawberries,
    and redcurrants
125g (4½ oz) caster sugar
zest of 1 lemon, cut into strips
1 tbsp orange juice
handful of mint leaves

METHOD
1 Place the mixed berries in a serving dish and set aside.
2 Mix the sugar with 120ml (4fl oz) water in a heavy-based saucepan. Heat slowly until the sugar has dissolved, stirring occasionally, then increase the heat, and boil for 5 minutes. Remove the pan from the heat and leave to cool, then add the lemon zest and orange juice.
3 Drizzle the syrup over the berries, then add the mint leaves. Leave to macerate for 10 minutes, before serving.

serves 4

prep 5 mins,
plus macerating
• cook 10 mins

Sweet lassi

There is no better way of cooling down after a fiery curry than with a glass of chilled lassi.

INGREDIENTS
500g (1lb 2oz) thick natural yogurt
300ml (10fl oz) milk
few drops of rosewater
1 tbsp caster sugar
4 tbsp crushed ice
few cardamom pods, crushed, to serve

METHOD
1 Whisk the yogurt, milk, rosewater, and sugar together until evenly combined and foamy, then pour into tall glasses over the crushed ice. Alternatively, put the ingredients into a blender and blend until frothy.
2 Sprinkle a little cardamom over the top of each drink. Serve at once.

serves 4

prep 5 mins

Paskha

This Easter dish from Russia is traditionally made in a tall wooden container, but a new flowerpot is used here.

INGREDIENTS

90ml (3fl oz) double cream

1 vanilla pod, split in half lengthways

1 egg yolk

45g (1½ oz) caster sugar

60g (2 oz) unsalted butter, softened

350g (12 oz) curd or ricotta cheese

45g (1½ oz) candied peel, chopped, plus
   extra slices to serve

45g (1½ oz) blanched almonds, chopped

45g (1½ oz) dark chocolate, chopped

METHOD

1 Place the cream in a small saucepan and scrape the seeds from the vanilla pod into the cream. Heat gently until hot, but not boiling. Beat the egg yolk with the sugar in a bowl, then pour in the cream and mix well. Allow to cool.

2 Beat the butter and the cheese together, then beat in the cream mixture. Stir in the candied peel, almonds, and chocolate.

3 Line the flowerpot with a double thickness of muslin. Put the mixture into the lined mould and place on a wire rack set over a dish. Refrigerate for 1–3 days to allow the whey to drain out.

4 When ready to serve, turn the Paskha out on to a serving dish, and decorate with candied fruit peel slices.

serves 4

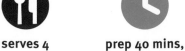

prep 40 mins,
plus 1–3 days
draining

prepare 1–3 days in
advance to ensure
proper draining

clean new 10cm
(4in) flowerpot
• muslin

Lemon and praline meringue

Impressive to serve at dinner parties,
but quite easy to make.

INGREDIENTS

3 egg whites
pinch of salt
175g (6 oz) caster sugar

For the praline

60g (2 oz) granulated sugar
60g (2 oz) whole blanched almonds
pinch of cream of tartar

For the filling

150ml (5fl oz) double cream
3 tbsp lemon curd
85g (3 oz) dark chocolate

METHOD

1 Preheat the oven to 130°C (250°F/Gas ½) and line a large baking tray with
  greaseproof paper.
2 Whisk the egg whites with the salt, until stiff but not dry. Add 2 tablespoons of sugar,
  and whisk again until smooth and shiny. Continue to add sugar, 1 tablespoon at a time,
  whisking well after each addition. Spoon into a piping bag with a star nozzle attached,
  and pipe six 10cm (4in) diameter circles on to the baking-parchment lined tray
  (see p11). Bake for 1 hour 30 minutes, or until crisp.
3 Meanwhile, make the praline. Oil a baking tray and put the sugar, almonds, and cream
  of tartar into a small, heavy saucepan. Set the pan over a gentle heat and stir until the
  sugar dissolves. Boil until the syrup turns golden, then pour out on to the greased
  baking tray. Leave until completely cold, then coarsely chop.
4 When ready to serve, whip the cream until just holding a trail, and fold in the lemon
  curd. Melt the chocolate in a heatproof bowl over a pan of gently simmering water.
  Don't allow the bowl to touch the water (see p13). Spread each meringue with a
  little chocolate. Allow to set, then pile the lemon curd cream on top, sprinkle with
  praline, and serve.

serves 6

prep 35 mins
• cook 1 hr
30 mins

piping bag
and star nozzle

Red fruit terrine

All the flavours of summer are wrapped up in this stunning red berry terrine.

INGREDIENTS

75g (2½ oz) caster sugar
90ml (3fl oz) elderflower cordial
juice of 1 lemon
2 tbsp powdered gelatine
225g (8 oz) raspberries

115g (4 oz) redcurrants
140g (5 oz) blueberries
225g (8 oz) ripe strawberries, quartered
extra fruit, to decorate

METHOD

1 Place the sugar in a saucepan with 450ml (15fl oz) water. Heat gently until the sugar has dissolved. Bring to the boil and boil the sugar mixture for 1–2 minutes. Cool slightly then stir in the elderflower cordial and the lemon juice.

2 Place 4 tablespoons of warm water into a small bowl and sprinkle the gelatine over. Leave to soak for 2 minutes. Place the bowl in a pan of hot water and stir until the gelatine has dissolved. Stir into the syrup.

3 Place the non-stick loaf tin into a roasting tin. Pack crushed ice halfway up the sides of the roasting tin and pour a little water over the ice. Scatter the raspberries into the bottom of the loaf tin and pour over enough elderflower syrup to cover. Allow to set.

4 Scatter the redcurrants and blueberries over the rasbesrry layer and pour over enough elderflower syrup to cover. Allow to set. Finally, scatter the strawberries over and pour in the remaining syrup. Transfer the roasting tin to the fridge and chill for at least 3 hours, or preferably overnight, until set.

5 To turn out, dip the loaf tin into hot water for few seconds and invert onto a plate. Carefully remove the loaf tin. Decorate with extra fruit.

serves 4–6

prep 45 mins, plus chilling • cook 5 mins

chill for at least 3 hrs, or overnight if possible

900g (2lb) non-stick loaf tin

Crème caramel

A French dessert with creamy, baked egg custard
and a golden caramel top.

INGREDIENTS

175g (6 oz) sugar
1 vanilla pod
600ml (1 pint) full-fat milk
4 eggs
4 egg yolks
60g (2 oz) caster sugar

METHOD

1 Preheat the oven to 160°C (325°F/Gas 3). Pour boiling water into the individual
ramekins and set aside. Fill a large bowl with cold water. Tip the sugar into a heavy
saucepan and place over a low heat, until the sugar has just dissolved. Dip a pastry
brush in water and brush the sides of the pan where any sugar crystals form. Increase
the heat and boil rapidly, gently swirling the pan until the caramel is a golden-brown
colour. Place the base of the pan in the bowl of cold water to rapidly cool to prevent it
cooking any further. (See p12.)

2 Working quickly, empty the ramekins and divide the hot caramel between them.
Gently swirl the dishes so that the caramel comes halfway up the sides of each
ramekin. Set aside to cool.

3 Using a sharp knife, split the vanilla pod and scrape out the seeds; place both the
seeds and pod in a saucepan with the milk, and heat until almost boiling. Remove from
the saucepan from the heat and discard the pod.

4 Meanwhile, whisk the eggs, egg yolks, and caster sugar together in a large bowl. Pour
the warm milk mixture over, whisking to combine, then pour into the ramekins. Place
the ramekins in a roasting tin and pour boiling water into the tin to come halfway up the
sides of the dishes. Bake for 25–30 minutes, or until just set in the centre. Remove from
the tin, cool, then chill until ready to serve.

5 Gently pull the edges of the custard away from the sides of the ramekin using a
fingertip. Place a serving plate over the top of the ramekin and invert on to the plate.

serves 4

prep 20 mins,
plus chilling
• cook 35–40 mins

4 × 200ml
(7fl oz) ramekins

Quick tiramisu

This luscious Italian dessert gets its name, which means "pick-me-up", from the espresso coffee.

INGREDIENTS
120ml (4fl oz) cold espresso coffee
75ml (2½fl oz) coffee-flavoured liqueur
350g (12 oz) mascarpone cheese
3 tbsp caster sugar
350ml (12fl oz) double cream
14 sponge fingers
cocoa powder, to decorate
coarsely grated dark chocolate,
  to decorate

METHOD
1 Mix the coffee and liqueur together in a shallow, wide serving bowl and set aside.
2 Put the mascarpone cheese and sugar in a bowl, and beat for a minute or two, until the sugar dissolves. Whip the cream in another bowl until it holds its shape, then fold it into the mascarpone mixture. Put a couple of spoonfuls of the mascarpone mixture in the bottom of a serving dish.
3 Dip and turn 1 sponge finger in the coffee mixture until just soaked, then place it on top of the mascarpone in the dish; repeat with 6 more sponge fingers, placing them side by side in the dish. Cover with half the remaining mascarpone mixture, then soak and layer the remaining sponge fingers. Top with the remaining mascarpone and smooth the surface. Cover the dish with cling film and refrigerate for at least 4 hours.
4 Sprinkle the top with cocoa powder and grated chocolate (see p13) just before serving.

serves 4

prep 20 mins,
plus cooling
and chilling

chill for at least
4 hrs

Pannacotta with strawberry purée

Strawberries are just one of the seasonal fruits that complement this creamy Italian dessert.

INGREDIENTS

½ sachet powdered gelatine

300ml (10fl oz) double cream

4 tbsp caster sugar

1 tsp vanilla essence

250g (9 oz) strawberries, hulled, plus
  extra whole strawberries to decorate

METHOD

1 Pour 2 tablespoons of water into a small heatproof bowl, sprinkle the gelatine over, and leave to stand for 3–5 minutes, or until it softens and becomes spongy. Quarter-fill a saucepan with water, bring to the boil, then remove the pan from heat. Set the bowl of gelatine in the pan, and leave until the gelatine dissolves, shaking the bowl occasionally.

2 Combine the cream and 2 tablespoons of sugar in another pan over a medium heat and slowly bring to a simmer, stirring until the sugar has dissolved. Turn off the heat, and stir in the vanilla, then whisk in the gelatine in a slow, steady stream. Strain the vanilla-flavoured cream into the moulds and leave to cool completely. Cover with cling film and chill for at least 3 hours until set.

3 Meanwhile, place the berries in a blender or food processor and blend to make a purée. Stir in 1–2 tablespoons of sugar to taste, then cover and set aside.

4 To serve, quickly dip the base of each mould in hot water. Working with one mould at a time, place a serving plate on top and invert, giving a gentle shake. Lift and remove the mould. Spoon the purée around each pannacotta and decorate with whole strawberries.

serves 4

prep 5 mins,
plus chilling

chill for at
least 3 hrs

4 × 150ml (5fl oz)
pudding moulds • food
processor or blender

Chocolate milkshake float

Children will adore this rich and creamy dessert drink, as it is made using all the things that they love.

INGREDIENTS

85g (3 oz) milk chocolate, finely
  chopped, plus extra flaked, to serve
150ml (5fl oz) boiling water
600ml (1 pint) milk
4 scoops chocolate ice cream
4 scoops vanilla ice cream

METHOD

1 Place the chocolate in a blender or food processor, add the boiling water, and blend until completely smooth.
2 Add the milk and chocolate ice cream and blend again until thick, smooth, and creamy.
3 Pour into 4 glasses and top each with a scoop of vanilla ice cream. Sprinkle with flaked chocolate and serve immediately.

serves 4

prep 8–10 mins

blender or food
processor

Strawberry semifreddo

This is Italian ice cream with a twist; texture and sweetness are added by crushed meringues.

INGREDIENTS

225g (8 oz) strawberries, hulled, plus extra whole strawberries and redcurrants to decorate
250ml (9fl oz) double cream
50g (1¾ oz) icing sugar
115g (4 oz) ready-made meringues, coarsely crushed
3 tbsp raspberry-flavoured liqueur

For the coulis

225g (8 oz) strawberries, hulled
25–50g (1–1¾ oz) icing sugar
1–2 tsp lemon juice, brandy, grappa, or balsamic vinegar

METHOD

1 Lightly brush the tin with vegetable oil, line the base with greaseproof paper, and set aside.

2 Purée the strawberries in a blender or food processor. Whip the cream with the icing sugar just until it holds its shape. Fold the strawberry purée and cream together, then fold in the crushed meringues and liqueur. Turn the mixture into the tin, smooth the surface, cover with cling film, and freeze for at least 6 hours or overnight if possible.

3 Meanwhile, make the strawberry coulis. Purée the strawberries in a blender or food processor, then press them through a fine sieve to remove the seeds. Stir 25g (scant 1oz) icing sugar into the purée and taste for sweetness, adding more sugar if you like it sweet. Flavour the coulis with the lemon juice, or other flavouring listed above.

4 Just before serving, remove the semifreddo from the tin, peel away the lining paper, and using a warmed knife, cut into slices. Arrange the slices on individual plates, spoon the coulis around the base, and decorate with whole strawberries and redcurrants.

serves 6–8

prep 20 mins, plus at least 6 hrs freezing

freeze for at least 6 hrs, or overnight if possible

20cm (8in) loose-bottomed springform tin • blender or food processor

freeze for up to 3 months

Caramel oranges

The sweet caramel sauce is a perfect match for the sliced fruit.

INGREDIENTS

4 oranges
225g (8 oz) caster sugar
crème fraîche, to serve

METHOD

1 Remove the zest from 1 of the oranges using a potato peeler; take care not to include any of the white pith. Cut the zest into very thin slivers and set aside.

2 Cut the zest and pith away from the other oranges. Slice the oranges, arranging them back into the shape of a whole orange, then place the slices in a mixing bowl.

3 Place the sugar in a saucepan with 150ml (5fl oz) water. Heat gently until the sugar dissolves. Increase the heat and boil for 8–10 minutes, or until the mixture turns a golden brown colour. As it boils, dip a pastry brush in cold water and brush around the inside of the pan to stop sugar crystals from forming. Slowly add another 150ml (5fl oz) of water to the caramel. Be careful (it will splutter a little), and stir to combine.

4 Stir in the reserved orange zest slivers and cook, stirring for 4–5 minutes, or until softened. Pour the syrup over the oranges and leave to stand overnight.

5 Serve each orange fanned out on a serving plate with a spoonful of crème fraîche. Drizzle with the caramel syrup.

 serves 4

 prep 10 mins, plus standing • cook 15 mins

 prepare the day before serving to infuse the flavours

Zesty lemon granita

Italians eat this as a refreshing sweet treat on a hot day, but it also makes a delicious dessert after a rich meal.

INGREDIENTS

6 lemons
115g (4 oz) caster sugar
twists of lemon zest, to decorate

METHOD

1 Set the freezer to its coldest setting and place freezerproof serving bowls or glasses in the freezer. Using a cannelle knife or lemon zester with a v-shaped cutter, thinly pare the zest from 4 of the lemons, and set aside, then grate the zest from the remaining 2 lemons, and set aside, separately.

2 Dissolve the sugar in 250ml (9fl oz) of water in a small pan over a medium heat. Increase the heat and bring to the boil, then boil for 5 minutes, or until it turns to a light syrup.

3 Pour the syrup into a shallow, freezerproof non-metallic bowl. Stir in the pared lemon zest and set aside to cool completely.

4 Meanwhile, squeeze the lemons to make about 250ml (9fl oz) of lemon juice. Remove the pared lemon zest strips from the mixture. Stir in the lemon juice and grated zest.

5 Transfer to the freezer for 1–2 hours, or until frozen around the edges and still slightly slushy in the middle. Every 30 minutes or so, use a fork to break up the frozen granita. Continue for 4 hours, or until the mixture has the texture of shaved ice, then leave the granita in the freezer until ready to serve. (See step-by-step technique on p7.)

serves 4

prep 5–10 mins, plus cooling and freezing • cook 5 mins

allow at least 4 hrs for freezing

shallow, freezerproof non-metallic bowl

freeze for up to 1 month

Espresso granita

Although light, this dessert has a delightfully heady character.

INGREDIENTS

100g (3½ oz) caster sugar
½ tsp pure vanilla extract
300ml (10fl oz) very strong espresso
  coffee, chilled

METHOD

1 Set the freezer to its coldest setting and place freezerproof serving bowls or glasses in the freezer. Dissolve the sugar in 300ml (10fl oz) water in a small saucepan over a medium heat. Increase the heat and bring to the boil, then boil for 5 minutes to make a light syrup.

2 Pour the syrup into a shallow, freezerproof dish. Stir in the vanilla and coffee and set aside to cool completely.

3 Transfer to the freezer. Every 30 minutes or so, use a fork to break up the frozen chunks. Continue to do this for 4 hours, or until the mixture has crystallized – it should have the texture of shaved ice. Then leave the granita in the freezer until ready to serve. (See step-by-step technique on p7.)

serves 4   prep 5 mins, plus   allow at least   shallow,
                cooling and freezing   4 hrs for freezing   freezerproof dish
                • cook 5 mins

Vanilla ice cream

Nothing beats creamy home-made vanilla ice cream
– you'll keep coming back for more.

INGREDIENTS

1 vanilla pod
300ml (10fl oz) milk
3 egg yolks
85g (3 oz) caster sugar
300ml (10fl oz) double cream

METHOD

1 Split the vanilla pod, scrape out the seeds, and put the seeds, vanilla pod, and milk
   into a heavy saucepan and bring almost to the boil. Remove from the heat, cover,
   and set aside for 30 minutes.

2 Beat the egg yolks and sugar in a large bowl. Stir in the infused milk then strain back
   into the pan. Cook the mixture over a low heat, stirring constantly, until the mixture
   thickens slightly and just coats the back of a spoon. Do not boil the mixture or the
   custard will curdle. Pour the mixture back into the bowl and cool completely.

3 Whisk the cream into the cooled custard. To freeze the ice cream by hand, pour the
   mixture into a freezerproof container and freeze for at least 3–4 hours, then whisk to
   break up any ice crystals. Freeze for a further 2 hours and repeat the process, then
   freeze until ready to use. To freeze using an ice cream machine, pour the mixture
   into the prepared freezer bowl and churn according to the manufacturer's
   instructions. This should take 20–30 minutes. Transfer to a freezerproof container
   and freeze until needed.

4 To serve the ice cream, remove it from the freezer 20–30 minutes prior to scooping.

serves 4

**prep 25 mins,
plus freezing
• cook 12 mins**

**allow at least
6 hrs for freezing**

**ice cream
machine desirable
• freezerproof
container**

**freeze for up to
3 months**

Eton mess

Culinary legend maintains that this medley was concocted after a schoolboy dropped a picnic hamper.

INGREDIENTS

350g (12 oz) ripe strawberries, sliced
2 tbsp caster sugar
2 tbsp orange juice or orange-flavoured
  liqueur
300ml (10fl oz) double cream
125g (4½ oz) ready-baked meringue
  nests

METHOD

1 Put the strawberries in a bowl, sprinkle the sugar over, add the orange juice, then use a fork to crush the mixture.
2 Whip the cream until stiff peaks begin to form. Crush the meringue nests into small pieces.
3 Stir the meringue into the whipped cream. Top with the berries and the juices, and stir together. Serve immediately.

serves 4

prep 10 mins

Cassata gelato

This type of Cassata uses one of Italy's favourite ingredients, ice cream, and is utterly irresistible.

INGREDIENTS

175g (6 oz) caster sugar

4 egg yolks

1 tsp pure vanilla extract

300ml (10fl oz) double cream, lightly whipped

60g (2 oz) glacé cherries, rinsed and roughly chopped

60g (2 oz) dried apricots, roughly chopped

60g (2 oz) dried pineapple, roughly chopped

30g (1 oz) shelled pistachio nuts, roughly chopped

200g (7 oz) fresh raspberries

METHOD

1 Place the sugar in a small saucepan together with 120ml (4fl oz) water, and bring to the boil. Boil rapidly for 5 minutes, or until thick and syrupy.

2 Whisk the egg yolks with an electric whisk, slowly drizzling in the hot sugar syrup, until the mixture is thick and pale. Fold in the vanilla and whipped cream. Remove a third of the mixture to a separate bowl, and stir in all the dried fruit and nuts. Cover, and chill until required.

3 Press the raspberries through a sieve to remove the seeds, then stir the purée into the remaining mixture. Pour into the larger mixing bowl. Place the smaller mixing bowl in the centre of the mixture, and secure in place with tape. (The raspberry mixture will be forced to rise up the sides of the pudding basin.) Freeze for at least 3–4 hours, or until firm.

4 Remove the tape, and pour a little hot water into the small bowl to release it. Spoon the dried fruit mixture into the centre, and level the surface. Cover, and freeze overnight.

5 To serve, dip the bowl into warm water for a few seconds, then invert on to a serving plate, and remove the bowl. Cut into wedges to serve.

serves 6–8

prep 25 mins, plus freezing • cook 10 mins

allow at least 24 hrs for freezing

electric whisk • 1 × 900ml (1½ pint) and 1 × 600ml (1 pint) mixing bowl

freeze for up to 4 months

Strawberry ice cream

Rich and creamy, this strawberry ice cream is enhanced with the tropical flavours of coconut, rum, and lime.

INGREDIENTS

400ml can coconut milk
200g (7 oz) white chocolate, chopped
150g (5½ oz) strawberries, hulled
4 tbsp icing sugar
300ml (10fl oz) double cream
2 tbsp white rum
finely grated zest and juice of 1 lime
lime wedges, to serve
strawberry halves, to serve

METHOD

1 Place the coconut milk and chopped white chocolate into a small saucepan, and heat gently, stirring occasionally, until the chocolate has melted. Set aside and leave to cool slightly.

2 Place the strawberries and icing sugar into a food processor and blend to a purée. Whip the cream to soft peaks, and fold into the coconut mixture along with the strawberry purée, white rum, and lime zest and juice.

3 Pour into a freezerproof container and freeze for 5–6 hours, breaking up the mixture with a fork every 30 minutes, or until firm. Scoop into balls, and serve with lime wedges and strawberry halves.

serves 4

prep 15 mins, plus freezing

allow 5–6 hrs for freezing

food processor • freezerproof container

after the initial freezing, freeze in an airtight container for up to 3 months

Coffee and pistachio parfait

A parfait is a luxuriously smooth ice cream, flavoured with a hot sugar syrup.

INGREDIENTS

1 vanilla pod
225g (8 oz) caster sugar
1 tbsp instant coffee granules
1 tbsp boiling water
6 egg yolks
4 tbsp Marsala

300ml (10fl oz) double cream
150ml (5½fl oz) Greek yogurt
125g (4 oz) pistachio nuts, shelled and
  roughly chopped, plus extra to garnish
rose petals, to decorate (optional)

METHOD

1 Lightly oil and line a cake tin. Split the vanilla pod, scrape the seeds into a pan, and add 100ml (3½fl oz) water. Stir in the sugar and heat gently until the sugar dissolves. Increase the heat and boil rapidly for 2 minutes, or until syrupy. Dissolve the coffee in the boiling water, and stir into the syrup. Set aside.

2 In a large bowl, beat the egg yolks and Marsala together with an electric whisk. With the whisk running, add the coffee syrup in a steady stream. Whisk for 6–8 minutes, or until thick and foamy, and at least doubled in size.

3 Whip the cream. Fold it into the egg mixture with the Greek yogurt and 85g (3 oz) of the nuts. Pour the mixture into the lined cake tin and scatter with the remaining nuts. Freeze for 4 hours, or until firm.

4 Dip the base of the tin into a bowl of warm water, then remove the parfait. Cut the parfait into squares. Transfer to a baking tray, lined with greaseproof paper, and return to the freezer until ready to serve.

5 To serve, place the parfait on chilled serving plates. Top each square with a scatter of pistachio nuts, and garnish with rose petals, if you like.

serves 8

prep 20 mins,
plus freezing
• cook 5–8 mins

allow 4 hrs
for freezing

20cm (8in) square
cake tin or plastic
container
• electric whisk

freeze for up to
3 months

Knickerbocker glory

A childhood favourite, with ice cream, fruit, cream, and sauce. It is traditionally served layered in tall glasses.

INGREDIENTS

2 peaches
8 tbsp strawberry ice cream sauce
8 small scoops strawberry ice cream
4 small scoops chocolate ice cream
150ml (5fl oz) double cream, whipped
1 tbsp sugar strands or sugar balls
4 maraschino cherries
wafer biscuits, to serve

METHOD

1 Place the peaches in a pan of boiling water for 30 seconds to loosen the skins. Drain and halve the fruit, discarding the stones, then peel. Cut the flesh into wedges and place a few into the base of 4 tall glasses or sundae dishes. Top with a scoop of strawberry ice cream and a drizzle of strawberry sauce.

2 Repeat the layering with the remaining peach slices, strawberry ice cream, and strawberry sauce. Place a scoop of chocolate ice cream on top.

3 Place a spoonful of whipped cream to one side of the chocolate ice cream and sprinkle with sugar strands. Decorate with a maraschino cherry and serve each with wafer biscuits.

serves 4

prep 15 mins

Mango sorbet

Juicy, fragrant mangoes make this sorbet a refreshing finish to a summer meal.

INGREDIENTS

2 large mangoes
200g (7 oz) caster sugar
juice of 1 lemon
1 egg white

METHOD

1 Cut the mangoes away from each side of their stones. Discard the stones. Make evenly spaced criss-cross cuts into the flesh of the mango halves, then bend each half backwards to separate out the cubes. Cut the flesh from the skin.

2 Place the mango flesh in a food processor and process until smooth. Press through a sieve and chill until ready to use.

3 Pour 300ml (10fl oz) of water into a saucepan, add the sugar, and heat gently, stirring occasionally. When the sugar has dissolved completely, increase the heat a little and bring to the boil, stirring. Boil for 1 minute, then set aside, and allow to cool completely.

4 Stir the sugar syrup into the mango purée, then stir in the lemon juice. Whisk the egg whites until soft peaks form, then gently fold into the mango mixture.

5 Pour the mixture into a freezerproof container and freeze for at least 4 hours, or until slushy. Mash with a fork to break up any ice crystals. Return to the freezer until solid. (See step-by-step technique on p8.) Alternatively, pour the mixture into an ice cream machine and churn according to the manufacturer's instructions. Transfer to a freezerproof container and freeze until ready to use.

6 Transfer the sorbet to the refrigerator for 15–30 minutes before serving. Scoop into serving dishes and serve.

serves 4   prep 15 mins, plus freezing • cook 10 mins   allow at least 4 hrs for freezing   ice cream machine desirable • food processor • freezerproof container   freeze for up to 3 months

Pistachio ice cream

The seed of an Asian tree, the pistachio nut has a hard outer shell with a distinctive soft green nutty centre.

INGREDIENTS

300ml (10fl oz) milk
½ tsp almond extract
3 egg yolks
85g (3 oz) caster sugar
few drops of green food colouring
 (optional)

175g (6 oz) pistachio nuts, shelled
 and roughly chopped, plus extra
 to decorate
300ml (10fl oz) double cream, lightly
 whipped

METHOD

1 Heat the milk in a heavy saucepan and bring almost to the boil. Stir in the almond extract.

2 Beat the egg yolks and sugar in a large bowl until creamy. Stir in the milk, then strain back into the saucepan. Cook the mixture over a low heat, stirring constantly, until the mixture thickens slightly, or just coats the back of a spoon. Do not boil the mixture or the custard will curdle.

3 Pour back into the bowl, stir in the food colouring, if using, and the pistachio nuts, and allow to cool completely. Fold the cream into the cooled custard.

4 To freeze the ice cream by hand, pour the mixture into a freezerproof container and freeze for 3–4 hours, then use a fork to break up any ice crystals. Freeze for a further 2 hours and repeat the process. Freeze until ready to serve. To freeze the ice cream in an ice cream machine, pour in the mixture and churn according to the manufacturer's instructions. This should take about 20–30 minutes. Transfer to a freezerproof container and freeze until ready to serve.

5 Remove the ice cream from the freezer 15 minutes prior to serving. Serve scoops scattered with chopped pistachios.

 serves 4

 prep 25–30 mins,
plus freezing
• cook 12–15 mins

 allow at least
6 hrs for freezing

 ice cream
machine desirable
• freezerproof
container

 freeze for up to
3 months

INDEX